# From the Ashes of Love

Mary Angeli Aguinaldo, M.D.

Presentation by *BookLeaf Publishing*

Web: www.bookleafpub.com

E-mail: info@bookleafpub.com

ISBN: 9789395271271

First edition 2022

# DEDICATION

For the ones who broke my heart,
You have taught me to be strong and gentle at
the same time.

# ACKNOWLEDGEMENT

I am grateful to BookLeaf Publishing for allowing me an opportunity to share my writing.

Thank you to my family and friends who continue to stay by my side through the years. You provide a solid rock I could always fall back on.

Thank you to all the people I have loved, and who have loved me. You may or may not be part of my life still, but know that you will always be part of my being.

# Wonderland

I took a tumble through Wonderland
And as I reached the woods, I felt a sudden sting
My dress ripped open and on my chest I found
The culprit that was making my nerves sing

Oh what a sight—what a terrible gash!
It bled and bled and would not stop
I tried everything, enchantments and ash
But neither spell nor herb could handle the job

Out of nowhere appeared, not a sliver of noise
No fade in his grin and laughing as he spoke
That cheshire cat with his mischievous voice
"Darling, why do you struggle against your soul?"

So I settled down on a field of daisies
Stumbled to the ground like a fallen cadet
With a last look at my body as my vision went hazy
I found the letters of your name written in scarlet

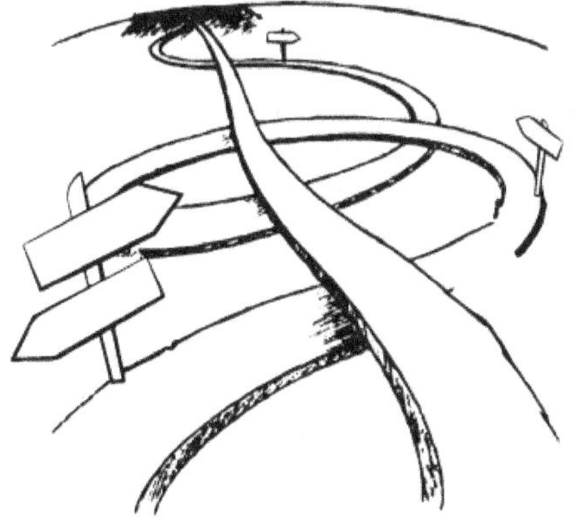

# August

August has come and gone again
And with it reminders of the past  we shared
That drive, that talk that signaled the end
The silence that followed that left me unprepared

I searched for hope between the lines
But your eyes left nothing more to be said
I can't pretend I didn't see the signs
That you had  left me way before then

When your skin tensed beneath my touch
And you broke our embrace with tenderness feigned
When you skipped our song, my heart plunged
And your voice quavered  another's refrain

When you said I love you from across the bed
Was it me you were lying to, or was it yourself
Helpless and crippled, should I have pleaded?
As I felt my soul stare at Death himself

Those old conversations inside my head
The trivial quarrels I thought we outgrew
Hours left waiting 'till the skies turned red
Tell me dear, when was the moment you knew?

Was it on that balmy August day?
The perfect paradox to our fruitless love
Every second, every detail I have replayed
As I search for answers from God above

Tell me when did my peace turn into chaos?
When my arms were once your sanctuary
Darling, there's  one last thing I ask now all is lost
When was the moment you stopped loving me?

# Waterfall

You once told me that you love me
Underneath the stars and skies
We drove upstate to the waterfall
And watched the waters echo our desires

In the dead of night you held my hand
Terrified as you whispered
Would I be like the others?
'Never,' I said, and kissed away the tears that
gathered

And now I watch the current flow
Alone with just your memories
I am but a drop in your waterfall
I will vanish, you will go on for centuries

# Unquenchable

Sage green eyes that pierced my wandering soul
Behind it a void, and I dove headfirst!
Her taste like sweet cherry set me aflame
But the fire burnt untamed, only dust resurfaced

Her porcelain skin as pure as my heart
The facade soon faded, so wide-eyed I was
A tender heart of gold, or so I thought
Yet behind the curtains, sharp were her claws

In the days after, I picked up the shards
Tried to seal all the cracks with glitter and glue
Yet the broken pieces no longer fit
And I'll never again be good as new

Love and pain, that's the nature of the world
The sun and the sea both watched as I cried
Still my love burns true with each passing star
Unquenchable amidst the rising tide

# How Far We've Fallen

I tried to stare down the shadows
As I struggle to say my  nighttime prayers
I've been dreading tomorrow
Because  it's one day further from where we were

Do you have a heart I can borrow?
Because mine broke down when you stopped to care
They say 'love and learn, you will grow'
'How?' when each breath without you is a nightmare

If I borrowed words from a poet,
"Isn't it amazing how far we've fallen?"
So can I just take a moment
To look back at all of the years you've stolen

I wore my armor and gauntlet
But your dagger pierced my very core
My bleeding wounds will never forget
Even as my body washes ashore

Now all that's left are dust and tears
I let myself burn while I stood my ground
And on my rebirth, I finally see
What we lost can never be found

# Drive

Same roads, same route, driving back upstate
I breathe in and out trying to block out your name
I imagine you laughing in my passenger seat
But today only love songs  keep me company

The birds still sing but I hear no melody
The lanes snake on  like the curves in your body
The harsh breeze stings like the last words you said to
me
The trees I pass, hollow as your eyes when you left
me

In allentown I stopped like we did that wintry day
The first time I said those words I was scared to say
Do you remember you said you would never change
That ours was a love that's here to stay

Now the air around me feels colder
The minutes, the hours, drag on forever
The clouds hug the hilltops, they remind me of your
caresses
As I ride alone with all your empty promises

I drive a hundred miles an hour
Thinking it might wake my dying heart
I could tell you I was headed home,
But where is home now you've left me on my own?

So I'll keep driving through every raindrop
I won't rest until you join me at the next stop

And when I reach the end of the road
Maybe your heart will beat for me once more

And you'll join me again on this journey
With your hand on my leg from across the car seat
Laughing at the way I slam the brakes
But until then I'll be driving in vain

I'll tell you the words to my favorite song
And you'll sing it with me like a beautiful poem
But until then I'll be driving alone
Waiting for the day you'll come back home

# Persephone

Be warned! That alluring lady in white,
Trust she will earn you nothing but spite
So came the warning bells from above
The message delivered by an innocent dove

But If loving you is a sin then i'd sooner be
Thrust to  darkness with the maiden Persephone
If loving you is a sin you can leave me be
On the river Styx and  I'll  swim willingly

For what good would life be without the taste of your
breath
If my arms never held your  delicate breasts
What good would life be sans this cross that I bore
Without a heart that loved so, that it beat no more

# Niagara

The great Niagara thunders
Over the rocky cliffs
In its glorious power,
It leaves behind clouds of mist

Flowing like curtains, dazzling and dangerous
Like your love so sweet and treacherous

Yet through the perilous waters I go
Vicious though  they flow
Through the falls and back
Even if it plunges my world to black

For like the rapids that could never be tamed
My love for you cannot be restrained

# Daffodil

I will write your name again and again
Till my hands go numb and are crippled with age
And if I run out of ink I shall write  it in red
And If i run out of trees I'll write on seas instead

I will write your name till the end of time,
Page after page, my muse, my daffodil
And in those spaces between the lines
Maybe there you will love me still

# The Other Side

What's on the other side of pain and tears?
Is there a field of boundless dreams?
Where love lasts forever and all souls heal
Where all wounds mend before they appear

Is there a garden that blooms in winter?
Filled with tulips, oh how the scent lingers!
Where the sun and stars dot the same sky
And no night emerges to break the light

Tell me what will I find on the other side?
A magnificent city built of sapphire?
Where the tree of life fixes all the broken
And one can find everything that once was stolen

Or Is there a woman dressed in white?
Waiting for me at the end of the line
And when she turns will I see your face?
Will she dance with me in stately grace?

Will you once again set my skin on fire?
Atop the mountain with your handsome eyes
Brighter than the streets with golden hues
For what good is heaven without you?

Fire and brimstone couldn't hurt me more
Than thought of eternity without you to adore
My love, no promise of salvation could ever do
For what good is heaven without you?

# Northern Star

When you sail on through the limitless sea
And discover what lies beyond the  horizon
Will you think of me afloat waters serene
Or when the curtains of mist are finally drawn

When you learn to use the wings you've always had
And realize just how high you can fly
Will you then return  to my faithful olive branch
Standing strong through the storms that have passed
by

When you find yourself and realize that I
Was the one you've been searching for all this time
When you find that the road you've been traveling by
For all its twists and turns leads you  back to my side

When you  finally  reach the ends of the earth
Follow the northern star and you'll see me anew
When at last you fathom all that you seek
I hope you'll find that I was one of them too

When you've searched your soul and you suddenly
see
That all along, we were destined to be
Come meet me at the meadow where we once basked
Beneath the sunlight and made plans so grand
And I will greet you with no questions asked
With a wreath of tulips upon my hand

# The Spaces Between

Every minute awake, and every night as  I fall asleep
And darling, even in those spaces between
In those moments unnamed, I think of you still

In the seconds after twilight and just before sunrise
In the realm between this world and the next lifetime
Darling, even in that limbo between hell and paradise
There in the land of the in-betweens, I will love you
still

In the narrow line between holding on and letting go
Between stubborn faith and losing hope
Between gratitude and pain
Between love and hate
There, my darling, I promise I will wait for you still

# Preface

I am a drop turned to vapor,
A withering leaf
You are the infinite river,
The forest that sustains me

I am a forgotten letter
A humble punctuation
You are the alphabet I speak forever
An  epic I will read for generations

One day, my dear, when the story is done
Maybe You'll stumble upon our page
Maybe you'll find my love was second to none
And that our forsaken chapter could have been your
preface

# Little Bird

Little bird so delicate
The world has turned you cold
You carry around all this weight
And let it hamper your beautiful soul

Little bird you came to me
Said you grew up without a clue
You asked "will you show me how to give,
and how to have a heart that's true"

So on my crown I let you rest
I sheltered you as you built your nest
Guided you to use those wings
Till you believed you can do all things

I gave you more than I could afford
Even when you didn't see your worth
Oh Little bird I loved you so
Faithfully through sun and snow

Now little bird how you've changed
You've grown tired of our shared space
My roots are too strong, my branches too short
And you wish my leaves were a different sort

So I'll let you go and pray you'll find
Whatever your sweet heart desires
Go and explore the starry skies
And worry not how high you fly

And when you grow weary and seek repose
When you lose your way  and you've strained your
bones
On the same ground, you'll find I still stand
Ready to catch you when you land

# Comet

I  wander the earth
In search of God knows what
I strive for rebirth
But can't let go of the past

I shoot for the stars
But I go out of turn
So when I hit my mark
My body starts to burn

You showed me the way
But I closed my eyes
Scared that if I stayed
I'd be blinded by your light

Now I'm lost in the galaxy
And you're lost in grief
We collided spectacularly
And I broke all your beliefs

Like a volatile comet
Terrified of the sun
Someday  you'll  write me sonnets
Of how I left you undone

# Time Turner

I found a clock that could turn back time
I was tired of tears and full of pain
So I turned the dial once, twice,  thrice
In hopes all this heartache I could erase

I greeted a younger version of me
In a place where you and I had never met
And in this place I had never lost sleep
Pining for love that I could not get

In this place there was no you
No struggle as you sought to push me away
No burning questions to pursue
Of what else I could have done to make you stay

Yet in my chest was a hollowness
At first my mind could not understand
What's worse than crying till you're out of breath?
Till I realized it's never having known love

So I'll throw my regrets despite our bitter end
For through this time warp, one thing is true
This beating heart has no scars to mend
Yet all it wants is to belong to you

# Thank You

Thank you for your love
Even if it was  a temporary love, the kind of love that
easily breaks
I know you loved me in your own way, the only way
you know how

Thank you for the lessons
I experienced so many firsts with you
And because of that, I get to look forward to all that
comes next

Thank you for your trust
When you were broken and insecure
I realized how much I could give without taking in
return

Thank you for the memories
I will cherish them forever
You made me cry like I've never cried before
But you also once made me the happiest person in the
world

And most of all, thank you for the heartbreak
You showed me just how strong my heart is
That it can shatter and still keep beating
Ready to love again

# Wishes

I loved truly, fearlessly
I gave freely, unreservedly
So I wish I could say, I have no regrets
That I couldn't possibly wish for anything more.

But I do.
Darling, I do.

I wish that I had enough time,
to show you that your past doesn't define you
to teach you to let go of your fears
so that you can open yourself up to love, fully.

I wish I had enough time,
to heal you and kiss away all your pain
to fix all the wounds you carry
to show you there is a way to be better.

I wish I had enough time,
to show you just how wonderful you truly are
And how much you deserve
all the most wonderful things in life.

# Love and Ashes

Laughter and pain
How quickly things changed

Faith and despair
Suddenly we're strangers again

Passion and rejection
It was the perfect misdirection

Promise and uncertainty
Left me ruined for eternity

Love and ashes
But I wouldn't change a thing.

# Incandescent

I can't tell you how
or when it started
I woke up one day
and my heart felt lighter

There was no reminder
of that fateful affair
A new scent lingered,
one of hope rekindled

She was like a beautiful storm
that came without warning
In a hail she  transformed
All my tears and my longings

She was like the sun that rose
at the end of the downpour
With her warmth she revived
All that's frozen in my core

She was like the star that shone
when the sky was darkest
Blazing a trail so clear
I followed with no protest

Like the storm that washed away
all rubble in its  path
Like the sun I could not escape
even if I tried
Like the star sent to save

the lost and the bypassed

You were the storm, you were the sun
You were the star, so powerful and grand
Your incandescence struck me in one glance
My sorrowful heart never stood a chance

# Phoenix

Ashes to ashes
But I'm not afraid
I'll glow in the embers
In a stubborn display

I am a phoenix
You are the flame
I'll let you consume me
And I'll be born again

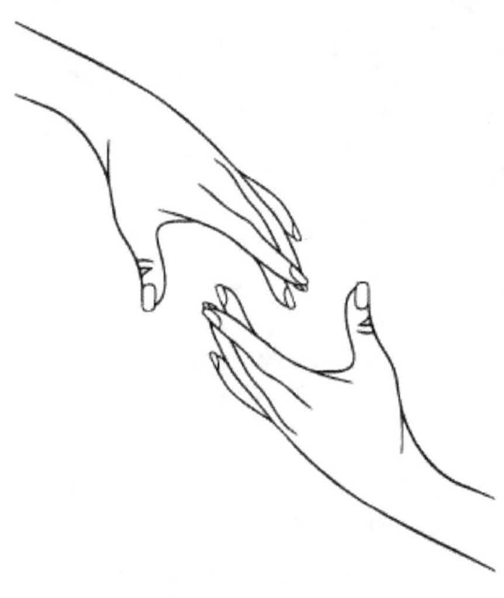